Crystal Meth
"The Miracle Drug"

The Miracle Drug Crystal Meth

T. Brian Loos

Published by T. Brian Loos, 2023.

While every precaution has been taken in the preparation of this book, the publisher assumes no responsibility for errors or omissions, or for damages resulting from the use of the information contained herein.

THE MIRACLE DRUG CRYSTAL METH

First edition. June 28, 2023.

Copyright © 2023 T. Brian Loos.

ISBN: 979-8223085799

Written by T. Brian Loos.

Also by T. Brian Loos

Say My Name Boy
Sir Ryan and Mark
The Miracle Drug Crystal Meth
Island of Men
My Straight Buddy
Post-WWII in Germany
The Prison Dungeon

By T. Brian Loos
Published by T. Brian Loos

This book is not meant to promote or glorify Crystal Meth use. It's about the history, what Crystal Meth is made of, how it affects our physical, mental, sexual and social health, the different ways it can be administered, recovery and withdrawal symptoms. It is also intended as a reminder, how this highly addictive and powerful drug changes and influences people's lives. It will be reinforced by the thoughts and experiences of two ex users at the end of this book.

But now here comes the surprising part, Meth can be also beneficial.

Meth, C10H15N, is classified as a Schedule II drug, that means it is allowed for limited medical use such as treatment for narcolepsy, attention deficit disorders and obesity. In 1887, amphetamine was first synthesized in Germany. Later in 1919, methamphetamine, also known as Ice or Tina , was synthesized in Japan. 1927 a chemist researched the effects of meth. He realized, it is increasing alertness and inducing euphoria. During WWII Germany, Japan and the United States gave their soldiers methamphetamine due to the energizing and antidepressant properties.

It was in Germany that the drug first became popular.

The Berlin based drug maker "Temmler Werke" compound onto the market in 1938.

A high ranking army physiologist saw in it a true "Miracle Drug" that can keep pilots alert and the entire army euphoric.

In 1939 the drug was tested on university students who were suddenly capable of higher productivity. From that point on, Germany's World War II army shipped millions of meth pills "Pervitin" to soldiers on the front, who soon gave it the nickname "Tank chocolate." British newspapers reported that German soldiers were using a "Miracle Pill."

But for many soldiers, the miracle became a nightmare.

They quickly became addicted. The side effects were sweating, depression and hallucinations. Not until the 1970s did West Germany's army remove the drug Pervitin from its medical supplies, and East Germany's army following in 1988.

Pervitin was banned in Germany, but the rise as an illegal drug had just begun.

The drug started to become popular again in the late 1970s in the US, when the Hells Angels sold Crystal Meth as a source of income and set up large drug labs.

They sold meth mainly along the California coast.

Meth was no powder in pill form no more, it was now sold in crystal form, and only few people knew how to produce these crystals.

That changed when in the mid 1980s a chemist in Wisconsin Steve Preisler, alias "Uncle Fester" published a drug cookbook "Secrets of Methamphetamine Manufacture." In this book, now in its eighth edition, Preisler published six different recipes for cooking meth.

All ingredients are legal, using a simple chemical reaction to extract the drug's main ingredient, Pseudoephedrine, found in cough medicine.

Combining it with liquids that increase its effectiveness, such as drain cleaner, battery acid or antifreeze, lye and lighter fluid. There were around 11,000 meth labs found in the US in 2010. Meth can be snorted, swallowed, smoked or injected.

Snorted it takes about 3 - 5 minutes to produce effects, smoked and injected immediately and swallowed about 20 to 30 minutes. IV and snorting, meth enters the body through the veins while smoking, it enters through the arteries. Meth users today consuming 1,000 times the dose soldiers in WWII took. The side effects are dangerous.

Meth weakens the immune system, which leads to skin problems, hair loss and "meth mouth" which means the teeth fall out and mucus membranes rot.

Meth users experience weight loss, loss of appetite and can develop kidney, stomach and heart problems, sleeplessness, elevated body temperature, paranoia, depression, irritability, anxiety, hallucination, for IV users HIV and Hepatitis C infections and infection of the heart

lining. It also alters the brain chemistry and the way meth users think and act.

That's why meth addiction is actually a brain disease.

Before and after pictures of meth addicts show, they look like living corpses within a short time.

But despite these side effects, meth remains as a fascinating drug and has lost none of the appeal to people who are using it long or short term. Even addicts who stopped using it are still fascinated by its powerful stimulating, euphoric high.

Worldwide there are around 24 million people and 13 million Americans that had tried meth at some point.

Meth is a very powerful stimulant of the central nervous system. It is easy to get, highly addictive and is one of the drugs that takes quite some time to recover from.

It is boosting the dopamine level in the blood up to five times higher than normal and about three times higher than Cocaine does.

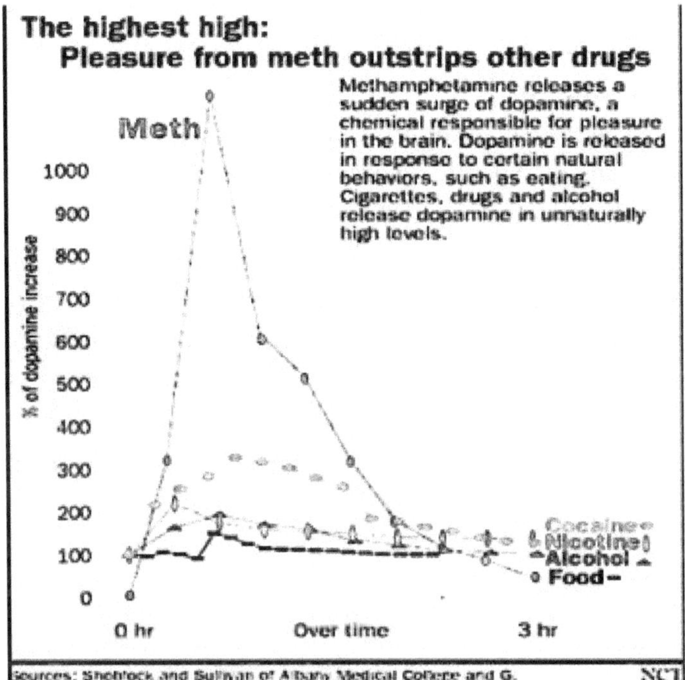

The highest high:
Pleasure from meth outstrips other drugs
Methamphetamine releases a sudden surge of dopamine, a chemical responsible for pleasure in the brain. Dopamine is released in response to certain natural behaviors, such as eating. Cigarettes, drugs and alcohol release dopamine in unnaturally high levels.
Meth
% of dopamine increase
1000
900
800
700
600
500
400
300
200
100
0
0 hr
Over time
3 hr
Cocaine
Nicotine
Alcohol
Food
Sources: Shotlock and Sullivan of Albany Medical College and G. Di Chiara of the University of Cagliari, Italy. Compiled by Dr. Richard Rawson, University of California, Los Angeles.
NCT

Dopamine is a neurotransmitter and is critical for the brain to control movements. Not enough dopamine means - can't move or control movements well.

Too much results in uncontrollable subconscious movements like twitching, jerking or repetitive movements. The heart is a muscle too, and too much dopamine results in increased heartbeat and blood pressure that can go as high as 190 – 160.

When dopamine is released it gives us a feeling of well being and enjoyment. Without enough dopamine, people feel the opposite, they feel fatigued and depressed.

Dopamine and other brain chemicals are stored in cells.

If something occurs like having sex or buying a new car for example, the brain pours out dopamine.

When the dopamine connects with the dopamine receptors, that is the moment when we feel good, it improves mood, self confidence and increases sex drive.

Meth destroys the receptors and we can't feel as much enjoyment no more.

Meth tells the cells to pour out dopamine until the body can break down the meth, typically after about 12 hours. The dopamine connects with the receptors and we feel high. As long as the user takes more meth, this process continues until there is not enough dopamine left to feel high.

At the end of a meth binge there is almost no dopamine left. That's when the user crashes and feels exhausted, severely depressed and unmotivated. It takes about 10 - 12 days for the body to produce and replace the amount of dopamine used while binging on meth.

It can take up to 18 month to have about 80% of normal dopamine levels for a recovering, abstinent long term user.

Meat, dairy, eggs, bananas and almonds are good sources of Tyrosine, which the body needs to produce dopamine.

Before we go further and talk about addiction, recovery and withdrawal symptoms, we want to ask ourselves, how much meth is too much.

A lethal dose of meth varies depending on purity and the user's weight, general health and tolerance. In 2013 the purity of meth was considered quite high, between 60 - 90 %.

Each person has a different tolerance to meth, so the amount to OD varies but a generalized guideline is:

Oral / eating, swallowing = > 0.15 g

Injection = 0.10 g or higher

Smoking or snorting = 0.05 g or higher

Common abuse doses are between

0.1 - 1.0 g a day.

A meth user can OD and not realize it right away. But in general, meth overdose is eventually leading to heart attack or stroke.

There are two different ways to OD.

Acute OD is when taking high doses and can result in harsh side effects, which can be very painful.

Chronic OD is when a user abuses meth over a long time, resulting in harmful physical side effects, temporary and permanent.

People with heart, thyroid and diabetes should not use meth at all, because these conditions may lead to sudden death.

At the beginning of meth overdose, the heart beats faster and the body needs more energy to keep up with higher body fluid production and higher body temperature.

Common signs of meth overdose :
Chest pain
Confusion
Dehydration
Dilated pupils
Hyperactivity
Hyperthermia
Rapid breathing
Stroke
Sweating
Irregular or fast heartbeat
High blood pressure

If you are with a person who OD, don't take actions on your own. Only medical staff knows how to treat overdose.

However, drinking water can prevent more dehydration and ice blankets can cool the body externally, special medication can control internal cooling.

Emergency room visits due to meth OD are up to 130,000 per year, 15 % were fatal.

Many fatalities usually have symptoms of coma, shock, inability to urinate and muscle twitching.

<u>Psychological complications from long term use are :</u>
Inability to sleep
Major mood swings
Delusional behavior
Paranoia
Violent behavior

How long does meth stay in our system, is another interesting question when we talk about this "Miracle Drug."

It stays much longer in the body than any other drugs.

For example, 50% of cocaine leaves the body after only one hour.

With a half life of nearly twelve hours, meth stays in the system for a much longer time.

It also depends on urine ph level, body mass, metabolism and amount of meth taken.

Peak blood concentration when swallowing meth occurs in approximately three hours.

For smoking and snorting, between two and three hours.

Meth can be found in hair month or even years after using it.

It stays in the blood for about 1 - 2 days, in urine 1 - 4 days, but heavy or chronic use can extend this time.

In saliva it can be detected 1 - 2 days after using. In sweat, meth is detectable within 2 hours of use and sometimes over a week after someone stopped using it. Meth in sweat leaves an oily residue on the skin and also a distinguished odor.

If someone would lick the sweat of the skin or drink the Urine, they would feel some kind of high, different though than from smoking or other popular methods.

About 40 - 50 % of meth taken, which was not broken down by the body, can be found in Urine. Taking baking soda dissolved in water before using meth, the Urine will turn basic and won't absorb the leftover meth the body didn't break down. It helps meth stay longer in the body but won't make it feel stronger.

Meth comedown - Here are the facts :

The Crystal Meth comedown is intense.

Typical signs are :

Excessive sleeping

Lethargy

Anxiety

Psychosis

Paranoia

Severe depression

The depression from meth comedown and withdrawal lasts longer and is far more severe than even cocaine withdrawal. Once a person takes meth, you want more, either to get high or to escape the meth comedown.

Once you take meth regularly, you can often sleep or eat like a normal person.

Meth comedown is not as dangerous as a heroin withdrawal, but it is still uncomfortable and many meth users continue using it to escape the withdrawal.

The Cravings:

The cravings for meth are very strong.

Someone starting out as a recreational user can easily become a full blown addict if they develop these strong cravings.

The Effects:

Many meth users say that they would never lie, steal or cheat to be able to use meth but all of that behavior eventually happens if their need for the drug becomes more important.

If you are addicted to meth you may:

Neglect family and friends

Neglect your job

Writing bad checks, committing fraud, selling drugs, continuing down the dark road that drugs create.

Cosmetic Effects:

"Before and after" photos of people prior to their meth use and during or after they have begun using it tend to be similar and shocking.

Meth mouth:

Brittle or missing teeth

Teeth grinding and tooth loss - collapsed jaw

Dry skin and gums

Missing or brittle hair

Sunken-in face

Are you addicted to meth ?

If you have at least one of these symptoms, chances are you are addicted.

Withdrawal symptoms as nausea, dry mouth, sweating, depression and extreme fatigue.

Dependency and tolerance to the drug:

Do you feel like you need it to feel better ?

To make it through the day or for any other reason ?

You use it again to counteract withdrawal symptoms ?

You lost control of your usage, using more than you planned or said you would ?

Your priorities are around your drug use, getting drugs, you have to have the drug in your possession to feel ok, you do whatever it takes to stay high incl. missing work ?

You keep using drugs even if you know they are hurting you. ?

Do you have mood swings, hallucinations or paranoia ?

Those are just the behavioral aspects of addiction to Crystal Meth. Physically you can expect even more symptoms.

Decreased appetite

Dilated pupils

Decreased or increased painful urination

Changes in sleep patterns

Irritability and agitation

Withdrawal timeline:

<u>Day 1 - 3</u>

Extreme fatigue, sleeping more than normal. Depression sets in.

<u>Day 4 - 10</u>

Strong cravings to use again begin.

Mood swings, difficulty to concentrate or getting motivated.

In some severe cases hallucinations, paranoia and anxiety may occur but should begin to subside after one week or so.

<u>Day 11 - 30</u>

Sleeping problems and lack of motivation. Severe depression and meth cravings usually continue.

<u>Day 31+</u>

Most users begin to feel better. Many of the withdrawal symptoms lift. Depression may continue. Cravings may come and go.

The following are the thoughts of two meth users before trying to stop using.

<u>Faces Of Meth Or Faces Of Death ?</u>

A "methed" up relationship

She is using a lot of names, but she is best known as Tina. First she shows her fun side when she is dating you, but she's always trying to get more control and power. You get engaged to see her more often and when she is finally married to you, she takes everything. Your friends, family, money, job, health and life.

Today I saw the police photo of my friend. I wish I never did.

It broke my heart to see him like this, bringing back memories, when I looked into his eyes and heard his voice for the very first time, saw his handsome face waking up next to me.

The same face I've seen today on the police photo, but still so different. Was it an accident or a desperate cry for help ? But it's not so easy to divorce her.

I don't think I can ever touch her again without seeing his face.

In his beautiful brown eyes, where I used to see his soul and spirit, I saw only her, the pure evil death. His left eye was half open, so was his mouth. Two of his teeth were missing.

Even right now, she's trying to convince me to give her another chance. But I just laughed at her.

She can feel my anger towards her, because she is still inside me. I can smell her on my skin.

He is now in a cold, isolated place, behind thick walls. The same walls that drove me crazy every night, keeping me separated from him, but sometimes we need these walls to protect us from ourselves.

I failed her game of domination once again, when I lost this protection and left that place called jail. At least he's safe, she can't do any harm to him while he's there.

He will clean up and gain weight again. I know he's a strong man. He can win the battle against the demons inside him, without them, her easy access to his heart & soul is no longer granted.

She will fight to regain power again, to continue her evil, destructive game. But her biggest fear and enemy is love.

So don't be afraid to show your love and support for somebody who is in desperate need of it to fight and win the last final battle.

Goodbye Dear Meth

I was in love with you for so long.

I thought you were the best thing that ever happened to me.

Whenever I needed you, you were always there for me and when you weren't I would feel like I was going to die.

I would search for you everywhere and nothing could stop me until I found you.

Sometimes you would show up when I didn't want you to. When I tried to quit you, you would find me every time and I would give into you.

Every time you made me feel like I was nothing without you in my life.

I gave up everything for you, but you just took every friend, relationship, job, self esteem, dignity, morals and freedom.

Well this is goodbye. I'm done watching you destroy myself and my friends.

I can see you everywhere in the eyes of people passing by.You're running the world, but you will no longer run my life.

<u>Health benefits of Meth</u>

Illicit meth is often used to self-medicate, according to Mark Willenbring, an addiction psychiatrist from St. Paul, Minnesota, with over 30 years of practice treating substance-use disorders. In Willenbring's experience, most of his patients who use illegal meth are treating undiagnosed ADHD.

"There's a high degree of comorbidity between substance-use disorders and ADD," Willenbring says. "They used meth for years in a controlled way, they never over-used it, they just used enough to get an effect, and then they stopped. One misconception is that it's always very addictive."

With most people who are addicted to meth, you can't tell it just by looking at them.

Carl Hart, a neuroscientist in Columbia University's Department of Psychology, agrees that the image of a snarling meth addict with bad teeth is a false stereotype. The dental damage so prevalent in anti-drug propaganda, he says, is more likely due to poor nutrition and lack of sleep—not to the drug. "There is no empirical evidence to support the claim that methamphetamine causes physical deformities," Hart wrote in a 2014 co-authored report.

There is a significant difference between these two opposing molecules. D-methamphetamine is what generally appears on the street—although it's often cut with other chemicals—whereas l-meth provides a less addictive, shorter-lived high that is less desirable among drug users. But people can and do use it recreationally.

Abuse is rare, however, in part because the high is shitty, but also because d-meth is so widely available. It's easier to buy a more powerful form of the drug on the street than it is to try to extract it from over-the-counter medications.

For J., the meth he's prescribed works better against his ADHD with fewer side effects than the Adderall he'd been on for 20 years. About five years ago, Jordan asked his doctor if he could try methamphetamine. The doc said sure.

The first time I brought it to the pharmacy, the pharmacist actually said to me, 'Oh, your doctor wrote this prescription wrong, this is the stuff that they make in meth labs," J. tells me by phone. "I told him to type 'Desoxyn' into the computer, and he did. He kind of backtracked, he obviously had no idea."

J. a middle-aged man from North Carolina who works in clinical research, now switches every three months between Adderall and Desoxyn to prevent building a tolerance to either stimulant.

Methamphetamine and amphetamine (one of the active ingredients in Adderall) are almost identical chemicals. The main difference between the two is the addition of a second methyl group to methamphetamine's chemical structure. This addition makes meth more lipid-soluble, allowing for easier access across the blood-brain barrier. Meth is therefore not only more potent, but also longer-lasting.

J. also doesn't feel "high" from the doses he takes—approximately 10 to 15 milligrams of meth per day. Doses at this level are well tolerated by most people.

It's very difficult to estimate the typical dosages of illicit meth taken on the street, but they are generally many times higher and taken every couple of hours. Further, the route of administration—typically, users smoke or inject illicit meth—allows for more of the drug to enter the bloodstream than taking a prescription pill.

At high doses, meth gives a rush of euphoria, boosting attention span, zapping fatigue, and decreasing appetite. Intense sexual arousal, talkativeness, and rapid thought patterns are also common. Body temperature and heart rate shoot up, which can cause irregular heartbeat, increasing the risk of seizures. If taken repeatedly over long periods, street meth can be highly neurotoxic, inducing paranoia and psychosis.

It's just a stimulant, like any other stimulant.

Part of the reason J. asked to try Desoxyn in the first place was to see if he'd develop any of the "stereotypical meth addict problems," as he puts it. He hasn't.

Those of us that know the reality have a responsibility to say, 'Hey, not that shooting up meth isn't bad, but the chemical itself isn't bad, J. says. "It's just misuse of the chemical that's bad."

Crystal Meth
Die Wunder Droge

By T.Brian Loos

Published by T.Brian Loos

© T. Brian Loos

2023

Dieses Buch ist nicht dazu gedacht, den Konsum von Crystal Meth zu fördern oder zu verherrlichen. Es geht um die Geschichte, woraus Crystal Meth

besteht, wie es sich auf unsere körperliche, geistige, sexuelle und soziale Gesundheit auswirkt, um die verschiedenen Verabreichungsmöglichkeiten, um Genesung und Entzugserscheinungen. Es soll auch daran erinnern, wie diese stark süchtig machende und starke Droge das Leben der Menschen verändert und beeinflusst. Es wird am Ende dieses Buches durch die Gedanken und Erfahrungen zweier ehemaliger Benutzer verstärkt. Aber jetzt kommt das Überraschende: Meth kann auch im medizinischen Bereich von Nutzen sein, wenn es in kleinen Mengen dosiert wird.

Meth, C10H15N, ist als Droge der Liste II eingestuft, was bedeutet, dass es für begrenzte medizinische Zwecke wie die Behandlung von Narkolepsie, Aufmerksamkeitsdefizitstörungen und Fettleibigkeit zugelassen ist. Im Jahr 1887 wurde Amphetamin erstmals in Deutschland synthetisiert. Später im Jahr 1919 wurde in Japan Methamphetamin, auch bekannt als Ice oder Tina, synthetisiert. 1927 erforschte ein Chemiker die Wirkung von Meth. Er erkannte, dass es die Aufmerksamkeit erhöht und euphorie hervorruft. Während des Zweiten Weltkrieges gaben Deutschland, Japan und die Vereinigten Staaten ihren Soldaten Methamphetamin aufgrund der anregenden und antidepressiven Eigenschaften. Es war in Deutschland, wo die Droge erstmals populär wurde. Der Berliner Arzneimittelhersteller „Temmler Werke" kam 1938 auf den Markt.

Ein hochrangiger Armeephysiologe sah darin eine wahre „Wunderdroge", die Piloten wachsam und die gesamte Armee in Euphorie versetzen kann.

1939 wurde das Medikament an Universitätsstudenten getestet, die plötzlich zu höherer Produktivität fähig waren. Von diesem Zeitpunkt an lieferte die deutsche Armee im Zweiten Weltkrieg Millionen von Meth-Pillen „Pervitin" an die Frontsoldaten, die ihr bald den Spitznamen „Panzerschokolade" gaben. Britische Zeitungen berichteten, dass deutsche Soldaten eine „Wunderpille" verwendeten.

Doch für viele Soldaten wurde das Wunder zum Albtraum. Sie wurden schnell süchtig. Die Nebenwirkungen waren Schwitzen, Depressionen und Halluzinationen. Erst in den 1970er Jahren entfernte die Bundeswehr das Medikament Pervitin aus ihren medizinischen Vorräten, und die Bundeswehr der DDR folgte 1988. Pervitin war in Deutschland verboten, aber der Aufstieg als illegale Droge hatte gerade erst begonnen.

In den späten 1970er Jahren wurde die Droge in den USA wieder populär, als die Hells Angels Crystal Meth als Einnahmequelle verkauften und große Drogenlabore gründeten.

Sie verkauften Meth hauptsächlich entlang der kalifornischen Küste.

Meth gab es nicht mehr als Pulver in Pillenform, sondern wurde jetzt in Kristallform verkauft, und nur wenige Menschen wussten, wie man diese Kristalle herstellt. Das änderte sich, als Mitte der 1980er Jahre ein Chemiker in Wisconsin, Steve Preisler, alias „Uncle Fester", ein Drogenkochbuch „Geheimnisse von der Herstellung von Methamphetamin."

In diesem Buch, das mittlerweile in der achten Auflage erscheint, veröffentlichte Preisler sechs verschiedene Rezepte zum Kochen von Meth. Alle Zutaten sind legal und werden durch eine einfache chemische Reaktion extrahiert.

Der Hauptbestandteil des Arzneimittels, Pseudoephedrin, kommt in Hustenmitteln vor. Die Kombination mit Flüssigkeiten, die die Wirksamkeit erhöhen, wie beispielsweise Abflussreiniger, Batteriesäure oder Frostschutzmittel, Lauge und Feuerzeugflüssigkeit. Im Jahr 2010 wurden in den USA rund 11.000 Meth-Labore gefunden. Meth kann geschnupft, geschluckt, geraucht oder injiziert werden.

Geschnupft dauert es etwa 3-5 Minuten, bis die Wirkung eintritt, geraucht und injiziert sofort und geschluckt dauert es etwa 30 Minuten.

Bei intravenöser Gabe und Schnupfen gelangt Meth über die Venen in den Körper, beim Rauchen gelangt es über die Arterien in den Körper. Heutige Meth-Konsumenten konsumieren das Tausendfache der Dosis, die Soldaten im Zweiten Weltkrieg einnahmen. Die Nebenwirkungen sind gefährlich.

Meth schwächt das Immunsystem, was zu Hautproblemen führt,

Haarausfall und „Meth-Mund", was bedeutet, dass Zähne ausfallen und

Membranen verrotten.

Meth-Konsumenten leiden unter Gewichtsverlust und Appetitlosigkeit und können Nieren-, Magen- und Herzprobleme, Schlaflosigkeit, erhöhte Körpertemperatur, Paranoia, Depression, Reizbarkeit, Angstzustände, Halluzinationen sowie bei IV-Konsumenten HIV- und Hepatitis-C-Infektionen sowie Infektionen der Herzinnenhaut entwickeln. Es verändert auch die Gehirnchemie und die Denkweise von Meth-Konsumenten.

Deshalb ist Meth-Sucht eigentlich eine Gehirnkrankheit. Vorher-Nachher-Bilder von Meth-Süchtigen sehen innerhalb kurzer Zeit aus wie lebende Leichen.

Doch trotz dieser Nebenwirkungen bleibt Meth eine faszinierende Droge und hat für Menschen, die es kurz- oder langfristig konsumieren, nichts an Attraktivität eingebüßt. Sogar Süchtige, die es nicht mehr konsumieren, sind immer noch von seinem kraftvollen, anregenden und euphorischen High fasziniert.

Weltweit gibt es rund 24 Millionen Menschen und 13 Millionen Amerikaner, die irgendwann einmal Meth probiert haben.

Das höchste Hoch:

Der Genuss von Meth übertrifft andere Drogen

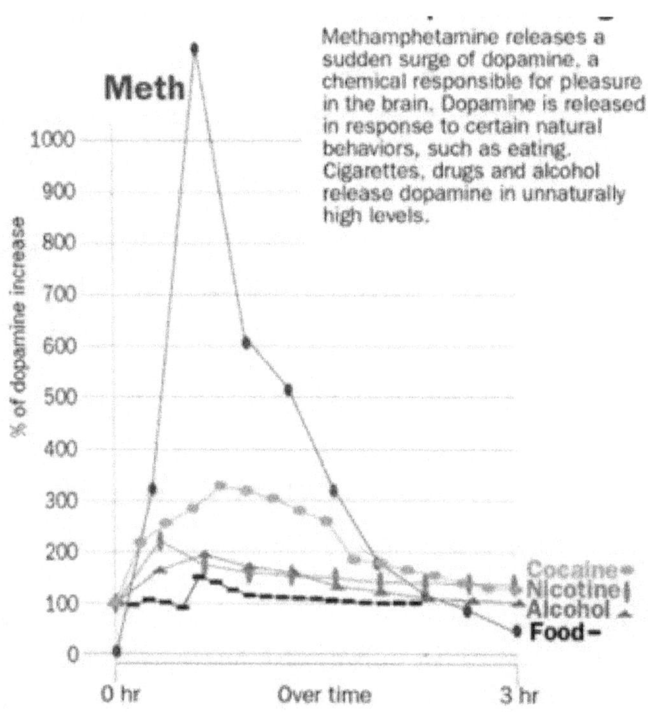

Methamphetamin setzt einen plötzlichen Anstieg von Dopamin frei, einer Chemikalie, die im Gehirn für die Lust verantwortlich ist. Dopamin wird als Reaktion auf bestimmte natürliche Verhaltensweisen wie Essen freigesetzt. Zigaretten, Drogen und Alkohol setzen Dopamin in unnatürlich hohen Mengen frei.

Dopamin ist ein Neurotransmitter und für die Bewegungssteuerung des Gehirns von entscheidender Bedeutung. Zu wenig Dopamin bedeutet, dass man sich nicht gut bewegen oder Bewegungen nicht gut kontrollieren kann.

Zu viel führt zu unkontrollierbaren unbewussten Bewegungen wie Zuckungen oder sich wiederholenden Bewegungen. Auch das Herz ist ein Muskel der solchen unregelmäßigen Zuckungen nicht ausgesetzt werden sollte.

Wenn Dopamin freigesetzt wird, gibt es uns ein Gefühl des Wohlbefindens.

Zu viel Dopamin führt zu erhöhtem Herzschlag und Blutdruck, der bis zu 190 – 160 ansteigen kann.

Die Ausschüttung von Dopamin gibt uns ein Gefühl des Wohlbefindens und der Freude. Ohne ausreichend Dopamin verspüren die Menschen das Gegenteil: Sie fühlen sich müde und deprimiert.

Dopamin und andere Gehirnchemikalien werden in Zellen gespeichert. Wenn etwas besonderes passiert, zum Beispiel Sex haben oder ein neues Auto kaufen wird Dopamin ausgeschüttet und man fühlt sich gut.

Wenn sich Dopamin mit den Dopaminrezeptoren verbindet, verbessert sich in dem Moment, in dem wir uns gut fühlen, die Stimmung, das Selbstvertrauen und der Sexualtrieb.

Meth zerstört die Rezeptoren und wir können nicht mehr so viel Genuss verspüren.

Meth fordert die Zellen auf, Dopamin auszuschütten, bis der Körper brechen kann

Das Meth abbauen, dauert normalerweise etwa 12 - 24 Stunden. Das Dopamin verbindet sich mit den Rezeptoren und wir fühlen uns high. Solange der Konsument mehr Meth nimmt, versucht der Körper mehr Dopamin zu produzieren.

Dieser Prozess setzt sich fort, bis nicht mehr genügend Dopamin zum gut fühlen übrig ist.

Am Ende eines Meth-Rauschs ist fast kein Dopamin mehr vorhanden. Dann stürzt der Benutzer ab und fühlt sich erschöpft, schwer deprimiert und unmotiviert.

Es dauert etwa 10 bis 12 Tage, bis der Körper die Menge an Dopamin produziert und ersetzt, die beim Meth-Konsum verbraucht wird.

Bei einem genesenden, abstinenten Langzeitkonsumenten kann es bis zu 18 Monate dauern, bis etwa 80 % des normalen Dopaminspiegels erreicht sind.

Fleisch, Milchprodukte, Eier, Bananen und Mandeln sind gute Quellen für Tyrosin, das der Körper zur Produktion von Dopamin benötigt.

Bevor wir weitergehen und über Sucht, Genesung und Entzugserscheinungen sprechen, wollen wir uns fragen, wie viel Meth ist zu viel.

Eine tödliche Meth-Dosis variiert je nach Reinheit und Gewicht, allgemeinem Gesundheitszustand und Verträglichkeit. Im Jahr 2013 betrug die Reinheit von Meth zwischen 60 - 90 %.

Jeder Mensch hat eine unterschiedliche Toleranz gegenüber Meth, daher variiert die Menge um zu OD.

Eine allgemeine Richtlinie lautet:

Oral/Essen, Schlucken => 0,15 g

Injektion = 0,10 g oder mehr

Rauchen oder Schnupfen = 0,05 g oder mehr. Übliche Missbrauchsdosen liegen zwischen 0,1-1,0 g pro Tag.

Ein Meth-Konsument kann überdosieren ohne es sofort zu merken. Aber im allgemeinen führt eine Überdosierung von Meth schließlich zu einem Herzinfarkt oder Schlaganfall. Es gibt zwei verschiedene Arten von OD.

Eine akute OD entsteht bei der Einnahme hoher Dosen und kann zu heftigen Nebenwirkungen führen, die sehr schmerzhaft sein können.

Von einer chronischen OD spricht man, wenn ein Konsument Meth über einen längeren Zeitraum hinweg missbraucht.

Menschen mit Herz-, Schilddrüsen- und Diabetes sollten überhaupt kein Meth konsumieren,

Denn diese Zustände können zum plötzlichen Tod führen.

Zu Beginn einer Meth-Überdosis schlägt das Herz schneller und der Körper benötigt mehr Energie um mit der höheren Produktion von Körperflüssigkeit und der höheren Körpertemperatur Schritt zu halten.

Häufige Anzeichen einer Meth-Überdosis:
Schmerzen in der Brust, Verwirrung
Dehydration, Erweiterte Pupillen
Hyperaktivität
Hyperthermie
Schnelles Atmen, Schlaganfall
Schwitzen.
Unregelmäßiger oder schneller Herzschlag und hoher Blutdruck.

Nur medizinisches Personal weiß, wie man eine Überdosierung behandelt. Allerdings kann Trinkwasser eine weitere Dehydrierung verhindern und Eisdecken können den Körper von außen kühlen, spezielle Medikamente können die innere Kühlung kontrollieren.

Bis zu 130.000 Notaufnahmen pro Jahr aufgrund von Meth-OD, 15 % endeten tödlich.

Bei vielen Todesfällen treten in der Regel Symptome wie Koma, Schock oder Unfähigkeit zu Urinieren und Muskelzuckungen auf.

<u>Psychische Komplikationen bei Langzeitgebrauch sind:</u>
Unfähigkeit zu schlafen
Starke Stimmungsschwankungen
Wahnhaftes Verhalten
Paranoia
Gewalttätiges Verhalten.

Wie lange Meth in unserem Körper verbleibt, ist eine weitere interessante Frage, wenn wir über diese „Wunderdroge" sprechen.

Es bleibt viel länger im Körper als alle anderen Drogen.

Beispielsweise verlassen 50 % des Kokains den Körper bereits nach einer Stunde.

Mit einer Halbwertszeit von fast zwölf Stunden bleibt Meth deutlich länger im Körper. Es hängt auch vom pH-Wert des Urins, der Körpermasse, dem Stoffwechsel und der Menge an eingenommenem Meth ab. Beim Schlucken von Meth tritt eine maximale Blutkonzentration nach etwa drei Stunden auf.

Zum Rauchen und Schnupfen zwischen zwei und drei Stunden. Meth kann Monate oder sogar Jahre nach der Anwendung im Haar gefunden werden.

Es verbleibt etwa 1–2 Tage im Blut, 1–4 Tage im Urin, bei starkem oder chronischem Gebrauch kann sich diese Zeit jedoch verlängern. Im Speichel kann es 1 – 2 Tage nach der Anwendung nachgewiesen werden. Im Schweiß, Meth ist innerhalb von 2 Stunden nach der Anwendung und manchmal auch über eine Woche danach nachweisbar.

Meth im Schweiß hinterlässt einen öligen Rückstand auf der Haut und einen charakteristischen Geruch.

Wenn jemand den Schweiß von der Haut lecken oder den Urin trinken würde, würde er ein gewisses High verspüren, allerdings anders als beim Rauchen oder anderen beliebten Methoden.

Etwa 40-50 % des aufgenommenen Meth, das vom Körper nicht abgebaut wird, finden sich im Urin. Wenn Sie vor dem Konsum von Meth in Wasser aufgelöstes Backpulver einnehmen, wird der Urin basisch und nimmt das übrig gebliebene Meth, das der Körper nicht abgebaut hat, nicht auf. Es trägt dazu bei, dass Meth länger im Körper bleibt

Aber dadurch fühlt es sich nicht stärker an.

<u>Meth-comedown – Hier sind die Fakten:</u> Der comedown bei Crystal Meth ist heftig. Typische Anzeichen sind:

Übermäßiges Schlafen

Lethargie

Aphistos

Psychose

Paranoia

Schwere Depression

Die durch den Meth-Abstieg und -Entzug verursachte Depression dauert länger und ist weitaus schwerwiegender als selbst der Kokain-Entzug. Sobald eine Person Meth nimmt, möchte sie mehr, entweder um high zu werden oder dem Meth comedown zu entkommen.

Der Drogenentzug ist nicht so gefährlich wie ein Heroinentzug, aber dennoch unangenehm und Meth wird von vielen Meth-Konsumenten weiterhin konsumiert, um dem Entzug zu entgehen.

<u>Das Verlangen:</u>

Das Verlangen nach Meth ist sehr stark.

Wer als Freizeitnutzer anfängt, kann leicht zum Vollnutzer werden.

<u>Die Effekte:</u>

Viele Meth-Konsumenten sagen, dass sie niemals lügen, stehlen oder betrügen würden.

Wenn sie Meth konsumieren, passiert dieses Verhalten irgendwann, wenn sie Meth dringend brauchen.

Denn die Droge wird immer wichtiger.

Wenn Sie von Meth abhängig sind, können Sie:
Vernachlässigen Familie und Freunde
Vernachlässige deinen Job
Uneingelöste Schecks ausstellen, Betrug begehen, Drogen verkaufen und den dunklen Weg weitergehen, den Drogen mit sich bringen.

<u>Kosmetische Effekte:</u>

"Vorher-Nachher"- Fotos von Menschen vor dem Meth-Konsum und während oder nach Beginn des Meth-Konsums sind in der Regel ähnlich und schockierend.

<u>Meth-Mund:</u>

Brüchige oder fehlende Zähne,

Zähneknirschen und Zahnverlust

Trockene Haut und Zahnfleisch. Fehlendes oder brüchiges Haar

Eingefallenes Gesicht

<u>Sind Sie Meth abhängig?</u>

Wenn Sie mindestens eines dieser Symptome haben, ist die Wahrscheinlichkeit groß, dass Sie süchtig sind.

Entzugserscheinungen wie Übelkeit, Mundtrockenheit, Schwitzen, Depression

und extreme Müdigkeit.

Abhängigkeit und Toleranz gegenüber der Droge: Haben Sie das Gefühl, dass Sie sie brauchen, um sich besser zu fühlen?

Um den Tag zu überstehen oder aus einem anderen Grund?

Sie verwenden es erneut, um Entzugserscheinungen entgegenzuwirken?

<u>Ihre Prioritäten</u>

Wenn Sie Drogen abhangig sind, verbringen Sie die meiste Zeit um sich Drogen zu besorgen

Sie haben die Kontrolle über Ihren Verbrauch verloren und mehr verbraucht als geplant

Halten Sie die Droge in Ihrem Besitz, um sich beruhigt zu fühlen

Arbeit verloren?

<u>Wie kann man erkennen ob jemand Meth nimmt:</u>

Verminderter Appetit

Erweiterte Pupillen

Vermindertes oder verstärktes schmerzhaftes Wasserlassen.
Veränderungen im Schlafmuster

Reizbarkeit und Unruhe

<u>Zeitplan bei Entzug:</u>

Tag 1-3

Extreme Müdigkeit, mehr Schlaf als normal. Depression setzt ein.

Tag 4-10

Es entsteht ein starkes Verlangen nach erneutem Konsum.

Stimmungsschwankungen, Konzentrations- oder Motivationsschwierigkeiten.

In einigen schweren Fällen können Halluzinationen, Paranoia und Angstzustände auftreten

Sollte aber nach etwa einer Woche nachlassen.

Tag 11-30

Schlafprobleme und mangelnde Motivation.

Schwere Depression und

das Verlangen nach Meth hält normalerweise an.

Tag 31+ Die meisten Benutzer beginnen sich besser zu fühlen. Viele der Entzugserscheinungen werden schwächer. Die Depressionen können anhalten. Heißhungerattacken können kommen und gehen.

Nachfolgend sind die Gedanken zweier ehemaliger Meth abhängiger aufgeschrieben.

<u>Faces of Meth or faces of death</u>

Sie verwendet viele Namen, am bekanntesten ist sie jedoch als Tina. Zuerst zeigt sie ihre lustige Seite, wenn sie mit dir zusammen ist, aber sie versucht immer mehr Kontrolle und Macht zu erlangen. Du verlobst dich, um sie öfter zu sehen, und als sie schließlich mit dir verheiratet ist, nimmt sie sich alles. Deine Freunde, Familie, Geld, Job, Gesundheit und Leben.

Heute habe ich das Polizeifoto meines Freundes gesehen. Ich wünschte, ich hätte es nie gesehen. Es brach mir das Herz, ihn so zu sehen und Erinnerungen wachzurufen.

Ich sah ihm in die Augen und hörte zum ersten Mal seine Stimme, sah, wie sein hübsches Gesicht neben mir aufwachte. Das gleiche Gesicht, das ich heute auf dem Polizeifoto gesehen habe, aber trotzdem so anders. War es ein Unfall oder ein verzweifelter Hilferuf? Aber es ist nicht so einfach, sich von ihr scheiden zu lassen.

Ich glaube nicht, dass ich sie jemals wieder berühren kann, ohne sein Gesicht zu sehen. In seinen schönen braunen Augen, in denen ich früher seine Seele und seinen Geist sah, sah ich nur sie, den reinen bösen Tod. Sein linkes Auge war halb geöffnet, ebenso sein Mund. Zwei seiner Zähne fehlten.

Selbst jetzt versucht sie, mich davon zu überzeugen, ihr noch eine Chance zu geben. Aber ich habe sie nur ausgelacht.

Sie kann meine Wut auf sie spüren, denn sie ist immer noch in mir. Ich kann sie

riechen auf meiner Haut. Er befindet sich jetzt an einem kalten, isolierten Ort hinter dicken Mauern.

Dieselben Mauern, die mich jede Nacht verrückt machten und mich von ihm trennten, aber manchmal brauchen wir diese Mauern, um uns vor uns selbst zu schützen.

Ich scheiterte erneut an ihrem Machtspiel, als ich diesen Schutz verlor und den Ort namens Gefängnis verließ. Zumindest ist er in Sicherheit, sie kann ihm in ihrer Anwesenheit keinen Schaden zufügen.

Er wird wieder alles in ordnung bringen und wieder zunehmen. Ich weiß, dass er ein starker Mann ist. Er kann den Kampf gegen die Dämonen in seinem Inneren gewinnen, ohne sie ist ihr der Zugang zu seinem Herzen und seiner Seele nicht länger gewährt.

Sie wird weiterhin kämpfen um ihre Macht zurückzugewinnen, damit sie ihr böses Spiel weiterhin betreiben kann.

Habe keine Angst deine Liebe zu zeigen für jemanden der sie braucht um den letzten Kampf zu gewinnen.

<u>Auf Wiedersehen, liebes Meth</u>

Ich war so lange in dich verliebt.

Ich dachte, du wärst das Beste, was mir je passiert ist.

Wann immer ich dich brauchte, warst du für mich da und wenn du es nicht warst, hatte ich das Gefühl, ich würde sterben.

Ich würde überall nach dir suchen und nichts könnte mich aufhalten, bis ich dich gefunden hätte. Manchmal bist du aufgetaucht, wenn ich das nicht wollte. Wenn ich versucht habe dich zu verlassen, du würdest mich jedes Mal finden und ich würde dir folgen.

Jedes mal hast du mir das Gefühl gegeben, dass ich ohne dich nichts in meinem Leben wäre.

Ich habe alles für dich aufgegeben, aber du hast mir einfach jeden Freund, jede Beziehung, jeden Job, jedes Selbstwertgefühl, jede Würde, jede Moral und jede Freiheit genommen. Nun, das ist ein Abschied. Ich habe es satt zuzusehen, wie du mich und meine Freunde zerstörst.

Ich kann dich überall in den Augen der Menschen sehen, die vorbeigehen. Du regierst die Welt, aber du wirst nicht länger mein Leben bestimmen.

Gesundheitliche Vorteile von Meth

Laut Mark Willenbring, einem Suchtpsychiater aus St. Paul, Minnesota, mit über 30 Jahren Erfahrung in der Behandlung von Substanzstörungen, wird illegales Meth häufig zur Selbstmedikation eingesetzt. Nach Willenbrings Erfahrung behandeln die meisten seiner Patienten, die illegales Meth konsumieren, nicht diagnostiziertes ADHS.

„Es besteht ein hohes Maß an Komorbidität zwischen Substanzstörungen und ADS", sagt Willenbring. „Sie haben jahrelang Meth auf kontrollierte Weise konsumiert, sie haben es nie übermäßig konsumiert, sie haben nur so viel konsumiert, dass eine Wirkung erzielt wurde, und dann haben sie damit aufgehört. Ein Missverständnis ist, dass es immer sehr süchtig macht."

Bei den meisten Menschen, die methabhängig sind, erkennt man es nicht einfach nur, wenn man sie ansieht.

Carl Hart, Neurowissenschaftler am Institut für Psychologie der Columbia University, stimmt zu, dass das Bild eines Meth-Süchtigen mit schlechten Zähnen ein falsches Stereotyp ist. Die in der Anti-Drogen-Propaganda so weit verbreiteten Zahnschäden seien eher auf schlechte Ernährung und Schlafmangel zurückzuführen, nicht auf die Droge. „Es gibt keine empirischen Beweise, die die Behauptung stützen, dass Methamphetamin körperliche Missbildungen verursacht", schrieb Hart in einem 2014 mitverfassten Bericht.

Es gibt einen signifikanten Unterschied zwischen diesen beiden gegensätzlichen Molekülen.

Auf der Straße kommt im Allgemeinen D-Methamphetamin vor – das häufig mit anderen Chemikalien gemischt wird –, während L-Meth einen weniger süchtig machenden, kürzer anhaltenden Rausch auslöst, der bei Drogenkonsumenten weniger erwünscht ist. Aber die Leute können es in der Freizeit nutzen und tun es auch. Missbrauch kommt jedoch selten vor, zum Teil, weil der Rausch beschissen ist, aber auch, weil D-Meth so weit verbreitet ist. Es ist einfacher, eine stärkere Form des Medikaments auf der Straße zu kaufen, als zu versuchen, es aus rezeptfreien Medikamenten zu extrahieren. Bei J. wirkt das von ihm verschriebene Meth besser gegen sein ADHS

Weniger Nebenwirkungen als das Adderall, das er seit 20 Jahren einnahm.

Vor Jahren fragte Jordan seinen Arzt, ob er es mit Methamphetamin versuchen könne. Der Arzt sagte sicher.

Als ich es zum ersten Mal in die Apotheke brachte, sagte mir der Apotheker:

Oh, Ihr Arzt hat dieses Rezept falsch geschrieben, das ist das was sie in Meth-Laboren herstellen. J. erzahlte mir telefonisch. „Ich habe ihm gesagt geben Sie „Desoxyn" in den Computer ein, und er tat es.

Er hatte offensichtlich keine Ahnung.

Meth kann hoch neurotoxisch sein und Paranoia und Psychosen auslösen.

Aber es ist nur ein Stimulant wie jedes andere Stimulant.

Einer der Gründe, warum J. überhaupt darum gebeten hat Desoxyn auszuprobieren war, um zu sehen, ob er eines der „stereotypen Meth-Süchtigen-Probleme" entwickeln würde, wie er es ausdrückt. Das hat er nicht.

Diejenigen von uns, die die Realität kennen, haben die Verantwortung zu sagen: „Hey, es ist nicht so, dass es nicht schlecht ist, Meth zu spritzen, aber die Chemikalie an sich ist nicht schlecht"

sagt J.. „Es ist einfach nur der Missbrauch der Chemikalie, der schlecht ist."

Don't miss out!

Visit the website below and you can sign up to receive emails whenever T. Brian Loos publishes a new book. There's no charge and no obligation.

https://books2read.com/r/B-A-DUVY-LCALC

BOOKS 2 READ

Connecting independent readers to independent writers.

Also by T. Brian Loos

Say My Name Boy
Sir Ryan and Mark
The Miracle Drug Crystal Meth
Island of Men
My Straight Buddy
Post-WWII in Germany
The Prison Dungeon

www.ingramcontent.com/pod-product-compliance
Lightning Source LLC
Chambersburg PA
CBHW061639130726
47996CB00003B/1376